NOV - - 2022

 **W9-CKI-019**

Llama

by Grace Hansen

Abdo Kids Jumbo is an Imprint of Abdo Kids
abdobooks.com

abdobooks.com

Published by Abdo Kids, a division of ABDO, P.O. Box 398166, Minneapolis, Minnesota 55439.
Copyright © 2023 by Abdo Consulting Group, Inc. International copyrights reserved in all countries.
No part of this book may be reproduced in any form without written permission from the publisher.
Abdo Kids Jumbo™ is a trademark and logo of Abdo Kids.

Printed in the United States of America, North Mankato, Minnesota.

052022

092022

Photo Credits: Alamy, Getty Images, Shutterstock

Production Contributors: Teddy Borth, Jennie Forsberg, Grace Hansen
Design Contributors: Candice Keimig, Victoria Bates

Library of Congress Control Number: 2021950540

Publisher's Cataloging-in-Publication Data

Names: Hansen, Grace, author.

Title: Llama / by Grace Hansen.

Description: Minneapolis, Minnesota : Abdo Kids, 2023 | Series: South American animals | Includes online
    resources and index.

Identifiers: ISBN 9781098261825 (lib. bdg.) | ISBN 9781098262662 (ebook) | ISBN 9781098263089
    (Read-to-Me ebook)

Subjects: LCSH: Llamas--Juvenile literature. | Pack animals (Transportation)--Juvenile literature. | South
    America--Juvenile literature. | Rain forest animals--Juvenile literature. | Zoology--Juvenile literature.

Classification: DDC 636.8--dc23

Table of Contents

South America

South America is filled with lovely landscapes, from rain forests to mountain ranges. Because of these special places, a **diverse** group of animals live on the **continent**. Llamas are just one of these animals.

4

North America

Europe

Asia

Africa

South America

N
W · E
S

Llamas

Llamas are not wild animals. They are domestic livestock. This means they are bred to help people.

Llamas are mainly **bred** in Peru and Bolivia near the Andes Mountains. Here, they help move goods over the rough **terrain**.

Peru

Bolivia

Llamas are large, sturdy animals. They usually weigh between 250 and 500 pounds (113-227 kg). They can grow to be 6 feet (1.8 m) tall.

Llamas are related to camels. Like camels, they have long necks and legs. They also have small heads and pointed ears.

Llamas are covered in **wool**.

Their wool can be gray, black, white, or tan in color. They can also have more than one color.

Food

Llamas are not picky eaters. They will **graze** on many kinds of grasses and other plants. They can also go a long time without water.

Baby Llamas

Llamas **breed** in the late summer or fall. After about 11 months, females give birth to one baby llama, called a cria.

Crias usually weigh between 20 and 30 pounds (9-13.6 kg). They can stand when they are one hour old. They will be fully grown by four years old.

21

More Facts

- Llamas are hard workers and smart. A 250-pound (113-kg) llama can carry about 110 pounds (50 kg) of supplies. If a llama has too much weight on it, it will refuse to move.

- Llama **pack trains** can contain several hundred animals. That's a lot of supplies being moved!

- Llamas usually have their **wool** cut once every two years. Their wool is water resistant, lightweight, and warm. It is used for making clothing.

Glossary

breed – to keep for mating or to come together to have young.

continent – one of the earth's seven major areas of land. The continents are Africa, Antarctica, Asia, Australia, Europe, North America, and South America.

diverse – of different kinds or sorts.

graze – to feed on growing grass.

pack train – a long line of pack animals carrying supplies.

terrain – land or ground, or the natural characteristics of its surface.

wool – the thick, soft, often curly hair of animals like sheep, goats, and llamas.

Index

Abdo Kids ONLINE
FREE! ONLINE MULTIMEDIA RESOURCES

Visit **abdokids.com**
to access crafts, games,
videos, and more!

Use Abdo Kids code
SLK1825
or scan this QR code!